It is a tree of life.

– Proverbs 3:18 –

All poetry is...making connections.

Robert Frost

To Debbie —

May God keep you
in his sight
and smile

Richard Morgan

HEBREW
LESSONS

Hebrew Lessons

Poems From my Jewish Heart

Richard Morgan
Paintings by Pat Morgan

ISBN: 1493750046
ISBN-13: 9781493750047

Library of Congress Control Number: 2013921176
CreateSpace Independent Publishing Platform
North Charleston, South Carolina

Edited by Jeanne Sutton

Published by Morgan House Press
Beach Haven, New Jersey

ALSO BY RICHARD MORGAN

I Am Sea Glass
A Collection of Poetic Pieces

Sea Glass People
Portraits in Words and Watercolors

Sea Glass Soul
Invisible Colors

For more information about these books
visit the author's website at
www.RichardMorganPoetry.com

For our children:
Jessica
Denia
Christine
And John

Poetic words
Are the children
Of
Head
And heart.

Contents

DEAR READER

I have written poetry for fifty years,
Been Jewish longer than that.
Along the way my poems
Recorded the wanderings
Of my mind as I climbed
My Mount Sinai, and
Prayed I hadn't missed
The Promised Land.

In this collection
Of my poetry,
I combine
The personal me
With the Jewish lessons
So many good people
Tried
To teach me.

I am blessed that I write poetry.
I believe there is poetry in everyone.
May you be blessed as well, and
Drawn to the blank page.
It is uplifting to find words,
Carefully selected,
Making visible,
A hidden part of you.

≈YP≈

YOUR PAGE

Between poems, several pages
have been left blank.
I call them "your page." They are
there for your words –
notes, thoughts, poetic lines and verse.
I hope their white space calls to you.

PART I

*For what is a poem
but a hazardous attempt
at self-understanding...*

Robert Penn Warren

PAST BONDAGE

Go ahead –
Quit, give up,
Go back to Egypt,
Be a slave. Worse,
Be a content slave.

The eternal struggle
Between a past
You can conceive
And a future
That's God's secret.

But the past has
No possibilities
For improvement.
Close that door and
Jump out the window.

Brave one,
You can fly.
Look back.
You have
Hero's wings.

SAINTLY MAN

Moses Dion was so saintly,
Other saints called him sir.
He was nearly blind and half deaf,
Yet people liked telling him their secrets.
He listened carefully and caringly,
Mostly for the tone of their voice,
Giving aid, but little advice.

When young muggers surrounded him,
Demanding his money and jewelry,
He gave them all he had,
A few coins from his pocket,
Then pointed out, he didn't
Wear a watch. Outraged,
One thug shot him twice for spite.

They ran away.
He lay there quietly.
His blood flowed freely,
Soaking the ground
That supported him.
His mind was calm.
He felt no pain.

He would have died
If not for a jogger, running a new route,
Seeing him and coming to his aid.
The good samaritan, an army medic
Familiar with gunshot wounds,
Stopped the bleeding, called
For an ambulance, and left.

Moses Dion, a saintly man, was saved.

REBUILD

Ashley was four years old
The summer I went to war.
She was an architect, engineer,
Builder of grand sand castles.
Detail and proportion
Were her expertise.

The first morning, her mother
Took her to the ocean's edge.
Ashley, armed with bucket
And butter knife, performed magic,
Creating a castle built
For a prince and princess.

After dinner, her grandfather
Escorted her on a walk to the beach.
She pulled his arm, hurrying him
Toward her creation. She found
The spot where her castle once stood.
Only a wet mound of sand remained.

"Why, Grandpa? Why?"
He pulled her close and hugged her.
What good was explaining
Wind and tides, sun and moon,
The eternal turning of the spheres?
But he tried.

She protested, "It's not fair."
He replied, "It's not trying to be fair.
It's just the way it is." He paused.
"You can build it again tomorrow."
She did. Again the tide took
Her castle. All summer long
She never stopped building.

I returned home, my year at war over.
I had lost buddies, others lost arms and legs.
I abandoned all hope of normal.
I spent my purgatory summer
Watching Ashley, now five, build,
And rebuild her sandcastles.

She never said it, but
She showed me:
Don't let the
It's-not-fair-it-doesn't-care
Beat you. Slowly,
She rebuilt my faith.

SOLOMON SPEAKS

A fool speaks,
Thinks later.
A sage thinks,
In silence.

A fool spills
Many words.
A sage
Conserves.

A fool talks -
The parrot.
A sage listens -
The sponge.

A fool
Rarely reads.
A sage
Savors poetry…

PARAMECIUM DON'T DO IT

Paramecium don't write poetry,
Rhesus monkeys recite no clever rhymes,
Neither knows much about alliteration,
At least they don't cheat or commit crimes.

They may not care about poetic license,
Or ability to compose loving verse,
They only do what nature's directed,
No debate if it's blessing or curse.

We preach the glories of the Ten Commandments,
Grope and gossip at an awful cost,
Bear false witness and covet our neighbors.
At least we delight in Shakespeare and Frost.

To avoid the pain of perdition,
We must find words of stillness and grace,
For I believe, with all my passion,
Poetry can save the human race.

CONCEPTION

I can imagine an evening
In October with its potbellied
Pumpkins and chilly nights.
My mother climbed the stairs
To her bedroom,
Shed her day clothes,
Donned a soft blue nightgown,
Studied her face in the mirror, sighed
Over new lines above her brow,
Slid into her side of the bed
Beside my father.

He was not asleep
Although most likely tired
From working late at the store.
Maybe, simply to subdue
The sensation of autumn in the air,
They came together
And were warm in each other's arms.
Something spectacular happened.
Months later, they'd try to recall
What night it was.

It was my night.
I can't conceive one
More important, even
Greater than my birthday.

Champagne! Fireworks!
Tell the world!
My ship is launched.

≈*YP*≈

≈YP≈

WOMAN - *SHECHINAH*

Womb of wisdom,
Birthplace of sympathy,
Teacher of tenacity
And tenderness,
Parent of prudence.

Look with approval.
I feel worthwhile.
Smile. I feel whole.
Your face is
My weathervane.

Men may train muscle
To champion a cause,
But the strength
To act with restraint
Is your girding gift.

INSIGHT

My house has
Windows and mirrors
Each made of glass.
Through my windows
I see people
Living their lives.
In my mirrors
I see only myself
Looking at myself.
The difference between
A window and a mirror
Is a thin layer of silver.
I lose a piece of myself
Every time I let silver
Come between me and
Seeing other people.

My house needs
More windows.

GOSSIP

Three people are hurt by
The gossiper's tongue:
The fool who listened,
The one described,
And the bird who sung.

COKE POEM

He died in Atlanta, age 100, surrounded, respected,
    admired.
Many years earlier, Coke's determination for beverage
    domination
Caused them to turn to him, Rabbi Tobias Geffen.
On the condition he never tell anyone,
They shared with him their secret formula, hoping
He would certify Coke as "kosher".
He identified two problematic ingredients;
They changed them without changing the taste.
His official endorsement, so revered,
Opened sales of Coke to Orthodox Jews throughout
    the world.

Now, Joseph, his great grandson,
Entrusted by the family to judiciously dispense
The Rebbe's ten thousand volume library,
Faced a Solomon-like task: how to divide the books.
I was Joseph's best friend before I moved away.
He invited me to join him in Atlanta during Christmas
    vacation,
Keep him company and keep him sane.
I did my best, in between meals with his extended
    family.
They asked me volumes of questions. I ate very little.

At the end of my visit, Joseph handed me
A beautifully wrapped thank you gift, telling me
Not to open it until I was home, assuring me
It was a modest token from the Rebbe's library.
We said goodbye, and I flew home to New York.

Back in my apartment, retreating to my favorite chair,
Carefully unwrapping my gift, I immediately saw
My new old book was a treasure, bound in
Timeworn leather and smelling of age. I fingered
Its cover. It weighed next to nothing. Slowly
I opened it. Gently I turned its tan pages.

Travel fatigue overtook me.
I was about to put it down when I noticed
A small slip of paper between two pages.
It looked so fragile, I dared not touch it.
The faded writing resembled a recipe,
A list of ingredients. Two had lines through them.

The phone rang, startling me. Closing the book,
I picked up the phone. My friend was calling
To thank me for my help. After I hung up,
I carefully placed the book on my shelf
Between other special volumes. That night
I dreamt the Rebbe visited me and
Whispered something in my ear.

If only I understood Yiddish.

DERRICK – MY GERMAN FRIEND

Derrick died without warning,
There was no time for goodbye,
My Fatherland friend and colleague
With a sadness in his eye.

He was born at attention
During an outrageous war,
Unthinkably, good Germans
Did all they could to ignore.

Through parents and two sisters,
He was tailored not for arms,
Schooled in language and culture,
Gentlemanly, peaceful charms.

He hoped that in America,
He'd move beyond all blame.
He told me of his secret,
That in bone, he still felt shame.

Derrick is home in his harbor,
While we are still out to sea.
In life he bore an anchor,
At last, he's finally free.

MY YIDDISH SAYINGS

I

A peacemaker
Must be
A magnificent
Liar.

II

A marriage
Will know more peace
If he's half deaf
And she's half blind.

III

We come from dust
And we return to dust.
If we're lucky, in between,
A dry martini with 3 olives.

BREATHING OUT

There comes a time when the doing stops,
The stride becomes a shuffle,
Distinguishing features,
Skin, height, hair, are lost,
Shrink, turn gray.
All that is left are the
Brittle bones of a being,
Once vibrant and
Accomplished, now
A human legacy,
Not yet dust,
But one
Only God or
A long-term lover
Could hold in their
Arms and
Cherish.
There is
No protest,
No whimper,
Nothing but
The peace
Of breathing
In, and then
Out.

STONES

Stones we wore on our fingers
Stones we passed on our journey
Stones so large they were a burden
Stones so heavy we worked together
Stones we gathered to make a wall
Stones we placed to mark our path
Stones we chose not to throw
Stones we used for a pillow
Stones shaped our dreams
Stones stand at our heads,
After.

I AM OLD, NOT DEAD

I am old
and want to be loved
as freely as
one loves an infant.

The infant smiles and
other people smile
back, his laugh
is considered music.

He can't do a
foolish thing, because
all his acts are
sincere and natural.

He soils his pants,
and it's okay,
they're replaced
without reprimand.

He is never
turned away,
especially in the
middle of the night.

He is held
when he cries,
gently stroked, when
in a bad mood.

I could be him,
If I wasn't
Strapped
To this chair.

BEING HUMAN

She said to the young man,
"You must be marvelous.
The moon follows you
Wherever you go,
The fall winds blow
The prettiest leaves
Onto your lawn,
And when it snows,
It turns the street
In front of your house,
Immaculate and white."
He looked at her eyes.
They smiled at him.
He smiled back.

I watched,
And yearned from my soul.
He should die.

≈YP≈

ENVY RUINS EVERYTHING

Ocean envies land
Striking it wave after wave
Washing it away
Resorting to tsunami
To soak it miles in.

Land envies mountain
Shaking it to its core
Quaking it till it falls
Loving each avalanche
It can cause.

Mountain envies sky
Blocking the light
Channeling the wind
Creating rain on one side
Desert on the other.

Sky envies ocean
Blowing hard over it
Whipping up whitecaps
Making unwilling waves
Crash against the rocks.

Ocean, Land,
Mountain, Sky
Were perfect
Before there was envy;
Envy ruined everything.

HOUSE OF A LIFE

Born innocent in the bedroom,
Trained to be clean in the bath,
Nourished and schooled in the kitchen,
Stole my first kiss in the pantry.

Married her in the living room,
Raised our kids in the nursery,
Dreamed my dreams in my office,
Retired in my sixty-fifth year.

Expired in my rocking chair,
Buried in my back yard,
Decayed in peace and made room
For the next, innocent owner.

GOD SMILED

What would you do
If God told a joke,
Lose all respect
Give your rabbi a poke?

What would you say
If God liked to laugh,
Double your doubts
Cut your faith in half?

What would you think
If God played hide and seek,
Decide he's for children,
The sick and the weak?

What might you confess
At heaven's heavy door?
"Oh God, I messed up,
Should have laughed a lot more."

DUST AND STARLIGHT

We humans,
Made of dust and starlight,

Shine like a beacon,
Smell of earth.

Will we forgive God?
Will we forgive ourselves?

We are born of divinity,
Fathered by eternity,

God's Sousa downbeat,
The spark in his eye,

Divine dust.

BERMUDA BLUE

Bermuda blue,
The water shimmers
Bermuda blue.
Bottle it, the blue disappears,
A gift from God, lost.

INDIA INDIANA

India, Indiana, no difference.
Dirty water or chilled dry wine,
Diphtheria or drunk driver,
When children die,
Parents are devastated by
The same heartless dagger.

They love their children,
Would die for them.
When children fall first,
All parents suffer,
Grief is a global disease,
India, Indiana, no difference.

≈*YP*≈

PART II

When a man
does not write
his poetry,
it escapes
from him
through
other vents.

Ralph Waldo Emerson

MY MOTHER'S GENTLE BROTHER

Why did we take the bus home,
Me, five, my sister, eight,
And Uncle Charlie?
It was only ten blocks, but
He said we had to. He rarely insisted,
Yet on this blue sky, cloudless day
He seemed anxious to get us home.

He had taken us for a walk,
Uphill, to Algonquin Park, where
Our parents never had time to take us,
A city park full of flowers, mowed grass,
And green benches. In the middle of our walk,
He lay down on one and said faintly,
"Let's stop. I need to rest."

After the bus ride home, he disappeared.
No one explained what happened,
But I remember that evening,
Seeing my mother in her bedroom,
With Dr. Zodikoff, our family doctor.
The door ajar, I saw her looking troubled
And sad. I wasn't allowed in.

Uncle Charlie never said goodbye.
We had no parting words,
But he knew words, he was a writer.
We share the same blood, the same
Love of written language,
And the memory of
Our day in the park.

SEARCHING

Early morning,
Alone with
Self-important gulls,
I walk the beach
Searching
For sea glass,
Hoping
For treasure,
Finding only
Fractured shells,
Sea stones
And frustration,
Wishing
I could find
Something
More whole.

At my feet
A clam – two
Soup bowls
Hinged,
Tightly closed
Protecting
An inner soul.

In my hand
Its hefty weight
Says *I am alive.*
I heave it
As far as I can,
Returning it
To the sea,
Feeling for the moment
Connected
And less
Alone.

AN IRISHMAN'S FAST

Yom Kippur, the Jewish day
Of soul searching, arrived.
My new wife told me I didn't
Have to fast, I wasn't Jewish,
But she would, sundown to sundown,
No food, no water, no coffee.
Her family was far away.
I was it. I couldn't let her
Do it alone. I'd fast too.

I started my fast by giving up
My morning hard roll and coffee,
Small sacrifice. I can do that.
As we entered her temple at 9 a.m.
She explained
Services would last
All day, into the evening.
Knowing this made it
That much more daunting.

The first two hours of prayers,
Mostly in Hebrew, I didn't understand,
Some, in English,
I tried to understand.
Then the Rabbi spoke.
I felt he was talking to me.
"Be humble," he said. "Acknowledge
Yesterday's transgressions,
Atone today, do good tomorrow."

By noon, my stomach wanted
To give in. *She's obligated, you're not.*
Find the nearest convenience store.
My stomach didn't understand
Marriage and commitment.
I needed to support her,
Especially where we were different.
Midafternoon was hardest –
The end still wasn't in sight.

After another hour of prayers,
Relief finally came.
I could no longer feel my stomach.
I had moved beyond hunger.
Hunger didn't seem to stress her.
She was calm, involved, quite serene.
For her, I put myself through this.
I didn't anticipate a spiritual experience
For me.

Then, for the second time,
In late afternoon,
The Rabbi spoke of repentance and
It reminded me of what my Mother said,
Almost weekly, when I was a boy,
"Do the right thing,
But if you don't,
Fast as you can,
Seek forgiveness."

At the end of the day,
When it was almost over,
I held her hand.
She looked at me
And smiled, her eyes wet.
As the shofar sounded,
I felt relieved and connected.
She knows I appreciate
Her Jewish ways.

As I stood beside her, an elderly man
Came up to me, thanked me for coming,
Asked me if I would like a schnapps.
Before I could say anything,
He took my arm and led me to a table
Where a gathering of old men stood,
Handed me a plastic cup of golden liquid,
Said "Drink." I did. *Ah, whiskey*.
He smiled. "Schnapps."

THE DOOR WAS ALWAYS OPEN

We were strangers;
They shunned,
Enslaved or expelled us.

We were outsiders;
They stole our homes,
Burned our books and scrolls.

They turned our ancestors
And grandparents
Into ash and dust.

Full of fear, they didn't know
They could not slay
Our hearts and souls.

Driven, we took with us
Our love of learning, laughter
And connection to God.

Our ways required
No luggage. They came along
Unnoticed.

EULOGY - RABBI ERWIN ZIMET

Erwin carried himself with gentle dignity,
An unobtrusive figure.
What he lacked in height,
He made up in stature.

His spirit, like breath on a frosty day,
Rose above the crowd,
Even Hitler couldn't diminish
The sparkle in his eyes.

He could lift with his wise words,
Inspire by the sincerity of his deeds,
Warm with his inner glow,
Light a fire by the intensity of his moral stand.

His convictions were vertical, like girders,
Yet he lived with both feet firmly on the ground.
He loved his wife, children, community;
Also sand and sea, all the beauty of nature.

He knew no other way to be, no other deeds to do,
No other words to say, no lesser love to feel.
His life, like a shooting star lighting the darkness,
Left a sweet, lingering afterglow.

BETWEEN 8 AND 80

— Youth —

"You're okay,"
An annoyed neighbor was saying.
"Go home to your mother,
She's waiting."
My knee throbbed, my blood dripped,
I knew the crack in the sidewalk
Was gloating as I limped home
Holding back tears.

— Years Later —

I came home from work.
My wife met me at the door.
"Your father called. Mom's
Not doing well. She won't make it
Through the night,
Just hanging on. Hurry.
Go home to your mother,
She's waiting."

— Many Years Later —

The bed I shared with my wife
Was soft and molded to our bodies.
This is not our bed. If I had the strength
I'd leave this place, but my love
Holds me so tight, whispering
"We're okay. It's all right.
Go home to your mother,
She's waiting."

≈*YP*≈

I HOWL

I howl
Because
That's all I
Can do.

I howl
Because
I'm flawed and
Can't accept it.

I howl
Because
I hurt and
Cause hurt.

I howl
Because
I see blood
That's not mine.

I howl
Because
There are wounds
That won't heal.

I howl.

LOCKED

An anemic red sun pushed itself
Over the shoulders of the horizon.
Walking the water-line, my mind unfocused,
I saw an old man standing like a lawn statue,
Watching the water, fishing with a kid's rod.
He wore a black yarmulke.
An oversized wool sweater hung on him
As if there'd been more of him at one time.
I approached. He turned his head,
Looked at me with dead fish eyes
And turned back to the sea.
I felt compelled to talk to him.

"How's the fishing?" was all I could think to ask.
He shrugged without looking at me, and,
With what seemed a German accent, replied,
"Same as usual. Lousy."
"What are you trying to catch?"
He didn't respond. I started to repeat my question
When he said "Lox. I'm trying to catch a lox,
But the bagel is the hard part."
I laughed.
"It's no laughing matter. I'm hungry."
"There are easier ways…" Facing me
He interrupted, "You think so? Life isn't so easy.
You couldn't understand."
"Maybe not. Try me."

"When I was seven I watched the Gestapo
Take my parents and sisters away."
"But not you?"
"I was hiding in the cupboard under the stairs."
He fell silent. Then,
"I didn't help them."
"But you were only seven."
"I heard my mother cry out my name
As they yelled at her to move.
All I did was hide."
"But you were only seven."
"Even a seven year old can hear.
Can know. Can remember.
I should have gone with them."

"Let me take you to the diner.
You can have lox and bagels
And tell me how you survived."
"Okay, I'll go with you.
But I'd rather have
A three egg omelet."

SISTER ANN

Ann was like the ideal aunt
The one to count on,
And over the years,
Many times I did.
With unfaltering faith
She cared about people.
Early on,
She cared about me.

Standing straight was her way
Of becoming a pillar
That held up heavy skies.
I could attempt any challenge
Knowing she was waiting
When I returned,
Wanting to hear my account
Regardless of the outcome.

I did not fear
What she might ask.
Her questions were insightful,
They added light, not fire.
She was always willing to listen
Without acting the judge,
Yet I often counted
On her good judgment.

Ann was not young, she was energetic,
Not imperial, she was influential.
She led by being there, caring so much,
Caring so consistently,
Never taking credit for a success,
But wanting you to succeed.
I feel sorry for anyone who never knows
Such an aunt as Sister Ann.

For Sr. Ann Sakac

SANTA AND SHIRA

The snow stopped
So Shira and her nanny
Went to the mall
As promised.
They waited on line
With the other good
Boys and girls
So Shira could sit
On Santa's lap
For the first time.
Shira slumped and slouched.
At five, patience was painful,
Squirming standard.
When her turn came
Shira hesitated a moment,
Then walked up to the roundish man
In the red suit and fake white beard.

He gently lifted her onto his lap.
He smiled, she didn't.
She told him her name.
"What would you like for Christmas, Shira?"
"I don't celebrate Christmas,
I'm Jewish."
Again he smiled, "Well so am I."
Now she smiled.
"Do you know any Chanukah songs?"
He asked.

"The Dreidel Song."
"I know that one. Let's sing it together."
They did, while the other boys and girls waited.
Satisfied, she moved off Santa's lap.
He winked at her.
Now they both were smiling.
Shira and her nanny started home
As it began to snow again.

GRANDPA SHERMAN'S CHANUKAH STORIES

I remember as a kid,
Each December, Grandpa told stories from his
    childhood
When Chanukah was a simple holiday.
Lighting candles, one the first night, two the
    second, one more
Each night until all eight burned so bright,
The bronze menorah ablaze in light. Prayers
    sung, stories told,
Old ones by the adults,
New ones by anxious kids old enough, finally, to
    take a turn. Songs
And clapping filled the air, chilly to save coal.
There were no gifts, no toys for the children, just
    gratitude at being together.
They'd watch the thin candles
Burn down, wax melting, dripping, pooling on
    the table. First time
We celebrated without him, my father
Cried softly as he retold Grandpa Sherman's
    Chanukah stories.

For many years he continued
The tradition, adding memories of his own. My
     eyes are so wet,
My heart so full, as
I tell you these stories, my Grandpa's stories, your
     Grandpa's,
Stories that will go
On and on.

MOTHER RUSSIA

From deep in my marrow
She cries, with her merciless winter
And frozen unyielding ground
Unable to harbor deep roots.
But I'll never call her home.

My Russian grandparents must have
Laughed lovingly with raw cheeks
Protecting a warm spot in their hearts
Thinking of their children, else
They never would have made love.

My American parents never spoke
Of a motherland, so I was silent too.
Their parents' frigid past failed to melt,
Passing on an unexplained thirst.
No stories of survival survived.

Yet, I am most certain they are there
In my soul's DNA. At the symphony
When the strings strike a minor chord
Or the horns blow a dissonant sound,
I respond beyond reason.

≈YP≈

ANGEL AT THE PUMP

There are angels in New Jersey.

I drop my wife off at Newark Airport,
Head home going north on the NJ Turnpike.
What makes me nervous is if I miss my exit
I'll be forced to cross the George Washington Bridge
Into the Bronx. No telling how lost I'll get.

In my angst I exit too soon
Into unfamiliar territory
And become hopelessly lost.
I am a man. I keep driving,
Can't bear to stop for directions.
I pass a downtown business district, drive
On to a suburban, residential section of town.

Tired and frustrated, I reason,
If I see a gas station I'll stop for directions,
But the station has to be on my side of the road.
This is asking a lot, considering
All I see are split level houses.
Then, out of nowhere, a Mobil station,
On my side of the road.

I pull in and approach
The lone attendant.
Sheepishly I ask,
"Could you help me? I'm lost."
He smiles, pauses, then replies,
"You're not anymore."
What a wonderful answer.
I am flooded with
Relief and gratitude.

In northern New Jersey
While hopelessly lost,
I met an angel.

THE PRINCE AND THE POET

He wants to:
Cure cancer,
Land on Mars,
Create world peace,
Have a wife and mistress,
Live brilliantly big.

I want to:
Cure my back ache,
Land on my feet,
Write a good poem,
Have a wife who's my friend,
Live quietly by the sea.

He's a prince
In his mind.

I'm a poet
In mine.

UNCLE MILTY AND ME

Uncle Milty,
A compact man,
Not really my uncle,
More a close friend of my parents,
Drove a New York City cab.
He had no kids and
A wife who didn't smile.
When they visited,
My mother's pot roast,
Served with little white potatoes
And yellow corn,
Prepared only for special guests,
Made Uncle Milty smile.
After dinner
He waved me closer and
I could smell the cigars in his shirt pocket.
I believed him when he cautioned me,
Catfish are really baby sharks,
He had no reason to lie.
Then, he gave me a quarter,
Told me to buy some candy.
I think he wanted one of us
To be happy.

NUTS AND DEATH

Nuts –
I said nuts,
Salty, crunchy.
Home, to me, is
Where the nut jar lives.
Cocktails at 4 with my wife,
We talk about our day over
Drinks and dry roasted nuts.
When I was a kid, my father kept
A bag of nuts from the 5 & 10 in his
Coat pocket. I recognized back then
The advantage of having one's own nuts.
Dad knew how to live. When I was 24, I was
The last one to see him alive. He died quietly,
Alone. I miss him. I miss the answers he never
Gave me to questions I never thought to ask. We
Were two peanuts inhabiting the same hard shell,
Unable to get through the divide that separated us.

BROTHERS

Brothers are like billiard balls
Banging against each other
Bing, bang no harm done,
Blood washes away,
Bones heal.

Insults and headlocks
Are common.
Mom, always there, ignores most.
Dad, at work, disregards by default.
Their silence encourages war.

Fraternal wrestling and competition
Are not forerunners of an adult need
For therapy. Brotherly dependence
Grows bonds, strong
As woven steel.

As for me, I bruise easily.
Heal slowly.
Realize now
My loss -
No billiard ball brothers.

KNIGHT DREAMS

King Arthur was wise,
Understanding,
And exceedingly bright.

Lancelot was young,
Full of himself, but
At least he was a knight.

They came after dark,
Woke me from sleep.
Said I could be their mate.

"Come now. Join us,"
King Arthur shouted,
"You'll have a noble fate."

"I'm nobody," I cried,
"While your exploits are
Terribly well known."

Lance scoffed, then snapped,
"There are lives to save.
Maybe you'll save your own."

When morning arrived,
They were gone, back to
Their glory and fame.

I was almost a knight,
Then I woke up, but
I'll never be the same.

≈*YP*≈

PART III

*There is a crack
in everything
God has made.*

Ralph Waldo Emerson

MOSES – TRANSLUCENT AND BLUE

Moses sits in the flap opening of his tent
Squinting against the blinding desert light,
Tired after forty years
Of royal responsibility,
Thinking about the future,
The tribes'. His.

The other side of the Jordan is the future
For the sons of the sons of Joseph,
But not Moses.
The men will cross first to face those
Who'll stand against Israel,
While he sits like a statue made of stone.

Beneath him, the sand is brutally hot
As is his inner turmoil.
He will not see Canaan.
God sentenced him to die soon
For using force when he was told,
"Speak and water will flow."

He's angry at the people,
Incessant complainers.
Angry at himself for his weak moment,
Angry at God's exalted expectations,
Angry at being angry.
Still, there's no relief.

He could argue with God,
But that won't change the outcome.
So Moses, the humblest man alive,
Sits as his anger slowly abates,
Waits quietly to close his eyes
On this side of the Jordan.

WOULD JESUS SIT

Would Jesus
Sit down with
Moses and
Mohammed?
Would their tears
Flow over
The way things
Turned out?

Would they hold
A newscast
Making a
Joint statement
Declaring their
Unity:
One world for
All mankind?

Or,
Would
They fight
And fiddle,
Over who
Sits
In the
Middle.

DUST

I am only dust trying to be a man
All I can do is the best I can.

I Am Only Dust trying to be a man
Sometimes I fought, sometimes I ran.

I Am Only Dust Trying To Be A Man
When I loved and lost, I loved again.

I AM ONLY DUST TRYING TO BE A MAN
I asked for help and God gave me a hand.

I am only dust trying to be a man…

ONE, NONE, ALL

Is God one
And we, another?
Or is God none
And we, just clutter?
Or is God all
And we, all too?
One, none, all,
Maybe, equally true?

ADAM

Born a man
Alone In Eden
With no past,
Unable to grasp
His morning reality:
Prickery plants,
Shapes moving
In the shadows.
He wonders
What is real,
The dagger of doubt
Or the consoling voice in his head?

Late afternoon,
Light begins to change,
He notices it before
He realizes it:
Shadows are fading,
Squinting no longer helps,
Something is wrong!
He can taste sweat
Dripping off his upper lip,
Feel his heart
Pounding
In his chest.

Night with its darkness
Brings on confusion,
Then panic.
He sits on the ground waiting.
Nothing this day prepared him
For the inexplicable blackness.
He thinks,
This must be death.
Lying down, he sleeps,
Dreaming for the first time.

When warm morning light
Wakes him,
Faith is born.

EDEN LOST

Before I
Was born,
I lived in my
Mother.
The
Sages say
I was taught
Wisdom there,
But when I left
The sanctuary of
My mother, I forgot all
I had learned. Parents
And teachers do not
Teach us, as much as
Help us remember.
Once, in a dream,
I recalled the
Way it was in
The womb:
Warm,
Refined,
All needs
Met. Now
I'm awake.
I wouldn't,
Even if I
Could,
Go back
To my Eden.

≈*YP*≈

THE EIGHTH DAY

On the eighth day,
Having rested,
Returning to view
All he created,
The spirit hovered
Over the water
Looking for
What still needed
To be done.
The sea said,
"I am deep,
I am wide,
I am mighty,
Like spring tide,"
So the spirit continued
Onto dry land.
"Are you in need?"
He asked. "No,
I am quite fine,
Contoured with hills,
A perfect design."
The spirit moved on
Until he came
Upon a garden,
Lush and green,
Home of man.

The spirit inquired,
"Adam, are you in need?"
Shivering in the morning chill,
Adam said, "I have no fangs
For defense, or
Legs fast enough
To run away.
I do not know, and
I greatly fear,
I will not last another day.
Am I your mistake?"
The spirit
Took pity and said,
"You must survive
On your own,
But you are never alone.
An angel will always be
By your side,
To gird you up
Or lengthen your stride.
Rally or run,
It will be your choice,
But if you listen
To your inner voice,
That will be me."
The evening of the eighth day
The spirit decided he
Had accomplished
All he had set out to do.

PASSOVER AND THE ELEVENTH PLAGUE

Pharaoh,
Lone survivor,
His multitudes of men,
Chariots and horses
All drowned,
Sits alone
On his golden throne
The morning following
His defeat, robe and hair
Still damp with saltwater.
"Is anyone here?"
The chamber is deathly still.

"Where is Moses?"
The walls remain silent.
"My slaves. What's
Happened to my slaves?"
The crickets in the corner
Do not answer.
"Where is Moses' God?
Tell him to show his face."
The invisible God
Does not respond.
"Weren't ten plagues enough?"
No answer.

"Am I to be alone till I die?"
Silence…

GOD

GOD did not expect to love us so much.

He made us look like his reflection
Lifting us as high as the angels,
But he did not expect to love us so much.

He gave us a mind to seek truth,
A heart to love each other,
But he did not expect to love us so much.

He was terribly disappointed early on,
Destroyed all except Noah with a flood,
But he did not expect to love us so much.

He made a covenant, a contract with us,
Gave us the rainbow as a sign,
But he did not expect to love us so much.

Why was he so hard on us,
His children?
He never expected to love us so much.

GENESIS OF DARKNESS

God did not create darkness;
It was there in the beginning.
His first creation was light,
And he saw it was good.
Was darkness not good?

Did darkness have
Such an ambiance
Of cold austerity,
That God felt alone?

Was Adam his answer,
To act the congenial
companion?

God's sidekick,
His

Tonto?

≈*YP*≈

PART IV

*The righteous bloom
and thrive.
They still bear fruit
in old age.*

from Psalm 92

BLOOD BROTHERS

When Cain killed Abel
He became a label
Warning with this fable
A lesson for all time.

He tried lying
Tearfully crying
Even denying
This was his crime.

Farmer vs. herder
Jealousy's murder
Nothing's absurder
Turning blood to brine.

Although so vain
Abel still loved Cain
Brothers just the same
Blood brothers of mine.

ONE TWO THREE GOD

Ruler,
Rock and
Redeemer,
Paper and scissors,
Life is not a game.
You give direction,
There is order,
An up and down,
Right and wrong.
You show me a solid place to stand
When the current is unruly and
I might sink below the foam.
You bring me back
When I have missed my turn
And desperately need a way home.
You tell me *be inspired* when I write
My story, my dreams, my poetry.
You bid me to cut out
The meaningless and marginal
Leaving the essential and eternal.
Since the sunset is not my artistry,
Nor can I make the moon rise,
All that is up to me is
Be in awe.
Be grateful.
Do good.
Breathe.

A PARABLE

Did I ever tell you the story
Of the baseball game between
The Devils and the Saints?

The Saints were first at bat.
Their leadoff man, Abe, swung
At the first pitch, but missed.
From behind him the Devil catcher,
In a low voice, said "You stink."
Abe wasn't sure he heard right.
He swung harder at the next pitch
And missed the ball by even more.
"I told you, you stink."
Abe's cheeks turned red
As he slapped at the third pitch.
Strike three. Abe was out.

The next batter, Ike, put cotton in his ears.
He hit a grounder on the second pitch,
Ran swiftly and was safe at first.
As he took a small lead toward second,
The Devil first baseman was saying something,
But Ike couldn't hear it. He took the cotton out.
The first baseman repeated, "You must be
The fastest runner I've ever seen."
With those unexpected words of praise,
Ike took an extra-long lead. On the next pitch,
He ran and slid into second. The ball arrived first.
He was out.

The third Saint up to bat, Jake, was
A man known for his wisdom.
Jake hit the first pitch. The ball sailed over the fence,
A homerun. After he rounded the bases,
He heard a voice booming from above.
"So tell me Jake, how did you do it?"
Reverently, Jake replied, "I could see
What the Devils were doing.
Abe forgot how good he was. Then Ike
Got a swelled head. As for me,
I prayed for you to be with me at bat.
You *were* listening weren't you?"

"Of course I was listening.
I'm always listening. Now,
About that homerun of yours..."

SATURDAY LESSONS

Saturdays at Grandpa Jacob's,
Sitting for hours in the sun,
We'd study Torah and the law,
Then sing Yiddish songs just for fun.

His lessons were very gentle;
Many times he made me laugh.
As I grew older he'd remind me
Moses held both book and staff.

The last Saturday I saw him
We sat together on his bench.
For a moment he stopped teaching,
Whispered, "All this means is,
Be a mensch."

LOST HUG

Rabbi Jack
Had my father's name.
He asked me to call him *Jack,*
It would never be comfortably done.
We grew close, but
Ran out of time.
He was 25 years my senior,
Accomplished and intellectual
With a sense of humor,
Loved a good joke,
But his serious side
Made him more
Moses-figure than man-friend.
We shared a handful of years and
A relationship that didn't
Have enough seasons to mature.
I was too shy to touch,
Let alone hug.
As with my father, after he was gone,
That's what I missed.

Last Saturday morning, Sabbath services
At the JCC we once shared,
Missing him
With a renewed feeling of loss,
I was given the honor,
In the sight of the congregation,
Of holding the Torah
With its new, royal blue cover.
It was heavy.
I held it close, felt it press
Against my chest.
Looking down
I saw, inscribed in the soft fabric,
Dedicated to Rabbi Jack.
I was hugging him after all.
I could feel his weight,
While he, in heaven, could feel
My arms circling him.
We joyfully embraced.

For Rabbi Jack Friedman

PROVERBS 31 REVISITED

A wise, loving wife is
A diamond in the sand.

Her husband knows
How precious she is and praises her.
He trusts her,
Confides in her,
And lacks for nothing.

No hour of the day,
Nor niche of the night
Is she not open to him.
Harshness
Is not in her nature.

She extends herself
To provide for her family's needs.
Like a thick woolen blanket
She keeps them warm
In a north wolf wind.

She rises in the dark. Her day is long,
Her light is on late at night. She is untiring.
Like the hummingbird,
She is always active,
Even when still.

She tends her garden
With skilled hands and nimble fingers.
The ground she touches turns fertile,
Her vines climb. She covers her family's table
With tomatoes and squash.

Her love extends beyond the family,
For as a plant turns its face to the sun,
She opens her heart to the deprived
And does not measure
What she gives.

Her strong, joyful beliefs
Make her a kind,
Sensible teacher
Sought out by many
For advice and direction.

Her husband thinks of her
Having the might and
Majesty of a mountain.
Her children feel safe in
The valley she creates for them.

Say the sages,
Youth lasts a moment.
Elegance is misleading.
But a wife in awe of God's ways,
She shall be praised for all time.

A wise, loving woman,
Is a diamond in the sand.

THIRTEEN ATTRIBUTES

Moses stares at the bush
Confused, wondering.
God answers him with -
A self-portrait.

"Who am I?
I am
Compassion,
Mercy, grace,
Patience,
Restraint,
Lover of truth and kindness,
Bearer of shortcomings,
Sin, and arrogance,
Judge and forgiver,
When possible,
That a future generation
Might survive
To be a covenant people.

I am your guide.
Be careful
Where you walk."

Moses, face to the ground,
Forces himself
To take a breath.

THE SINAI EXPERIENCE

The pale nothingness
Of the desert
Is an illusion.

Life is fragile and concealed,
Yet thrives in spite of
A sun-oven by day, and
A moon-freezer by night.
The light at noon is enough
To make a man
Give up his eyes,
And in the evening,
The eternity of stars
Obliges him to
Abandon his brain.
Burned and chilled
For forty years,
His survival
Such a miracle,
He begins to see
He is not on his own.

In this place,
A man could be molded
For an exalted purpose
By a God
Mighty enough
To align
The laws of nature.

SIN

In
gra
tit
ude -
The
Fir
st
Sin.

WAITING FOR THE TENTH MAN

While waiting for a minyan,
Harry's hand slides into his pocket.
He recalls a promise to his dead wife
As he fingers her broken gold locket.

While waiting for one more man
Myron reads about the patriarchs' lives.
What amazes him more than anything,
Their stories were shaped by their wives.

While waiting for prayers to start
Stanley, not subtly, takes a nap,
His breathing slows as he snores,
His glasses fall into his lap.

While waiting for the tenth man,
Rabbi looks out the open door.
He still sees a star in the east,
He decides to wait just a bit more.

While waiting to begin, nine old men
Nap, read or feel a sorrow,
With no minyan they stand and pray on their own,
Rabbi shrugs, "We'll try again tomorrow."

≈*YP*≈

ABOUT THE AUTHOR AND ARTIST

Richard Morgan grew up in Newburgh, New York, a small city 60 miles north of Manhattan. "I remember when I was in Sunday School, Mrs. Mansfield made us memorize the Ten Commandments. I don't recall any discussion of what they meant."

Richard continued studying through bar mitzvah and never stopped. His search took him beyond Judaism to other religious and spiritual philosophies. He lunched unforgettably with Huston Smith, the renowned author of *World's Religions - A Guide to Our Wisdom Traditions.* "Huston is wonderful example of humility housing greatness."

Richard's poetry is influenced by all he has learned. He has written for 50 years and has published a trilogy of poetry books: *I Am Sea Glass - A Collection of Poetic Pieces, Sea Glass People - Portraits in Words and Watercolors,* and *Sea Glass Soul - Invisible Colors.* Each book combines his poetry with his wife, artist Pat Morgan's paintings. Richard and Pat live on the Jersey shore where the winters are quiet except for the unrelenting wind. They cherish the solitary time for writing, painting and reading.

After 40 years in education as a teacher and administrator, Richard enjoys coaching personal poetry because he believes there is poetry in everyone. In his workshops, he encourages participants to write their feelings.

Pat is also a teacher. She shares a love of watercolor with her many students. They respond with rave reviews. When she is not teaching or painting, she is out in her gardens. The colors of her flowers inspire a soft palette for her art.

More of Pat's paintings can be seen at PatMorganArt.com.

Richard can be reached at
RichardMorgan Poetry.com. or
email: rsmorgan18@comcast.net.

HEBREW LESSONS

28530716R00075

Made in the USA
Charleston, SC
15 April 2014